Inexpensive Equipment for Games, Play, and Physical Activity

Inexpensive Equipment for Games, Play, and Physical Activity

Charles B. Corbin
Kansas State University
Manhattan, Kansas

WM. C. BROWN COMPANY PUBLISHERS
Dubuque, Iowa

Contents

Preface

Frequently teachers are surprised to learn, after four years of college, that the first day on the job is not what they expected. All too often they must "make do" with limited equipment which makes teaching difficult, especially when class size is very large as is frequently the case.

It is the purpose of this book to provide teachers, beginning and experienced, with some ideas for constructing "homemade" equipment which will make it possible to have some piece of equipment for each child, and so keep all children active and involved in the class experience.

In addition some activities are suggested for using the equipment. Some special activities, which I have found to be particularly interesting to children and easily adaptable to large classes, are also presented. Finally, I have offered practical teaching suggestions. It is hoped that this book will not only be of value to the classroom teacher and the physical educator but to scout leaders, recreation leaders and others interested in developing learning through play.

Special thanks go to David Corbin, Paul Shimon, David Reams, Miss Joyce Takacs, and Miss Kathy Seale for their suggestions and contributions to the book.

Chapter *1*

Introduction

Few people would question the desirability of having individualized instruction in physical education classes, especially in the primary grades. Unfortunately, large class size precludes the possibility of much individual attention for any given student. The problem may be compounded by the fact that many schools lack adequate equipment to allow children to "teach themselves" in these large classes. Too often the teacher will have one or two balls for thirty to forty students, or one ball and one bat for the entire class. In these situations the learner must be content to wait his turn "inactively."

The teacher can attempt to remedy the situation and allow for individualized instruction plus increased "active participation" for all children by taking advantage of special pieces of homemade inexpensive equipment. It is the purpose of this book to describe some of such inexpensive equipment as well as accompanying activities which are most practical for use in the elementary schools.

Use of Inexpensive Equipment in Movement Exploration

One of the hoped-for results of supplying each child with his own equipment is that he will be encouraged to give a creative response unique to himself.

There are many activities for which there is no single "best" way to perform a skill. The fact that each child is free to perform in his "own way" allows him to move within the limitations of his own potential. Movement problem solving, as in Movement Education and Movement Exploration, can be greatly enhanced as a result of greater availability of equipment. Most, if not all, of the inexpensive equipment described in this book is quite usable in movement education programs which emphasize the individual's unique responses to movement problems.

1

Cooperative Construction of Equipment

Most of the ideas for equipment construction are simple enough for the elementary school child to grasp so that the equipment could be constructed at home with little adult assistance. It is suggested that children be encouraged to construct items at home and bring them to school to be deposited for use in physical education classes and during free play. For example if each child made a "bleach bottle ball scoop" this equipment would be stored in a central location for use in classes. The same would be true of other pieces of equipment.

Another idea involves the cooperation of the physical education teacher and the classroom teacher. In this case items such as "Lumey Sticks" could be made and painted for art class, the origination discussed in history, and the actual activity could be learned during physical education. Similarly Nylon Stocking Rackets, Tin Can Stilts, etc., could be made in crafts classes. Only a few of the items presented in the book would require special construction by the teacher.

Book Content

The following pages will include instructions for constructing inexpensive equipment followed by some activities which require the use of the equipment. In many cases references are given which suggest additional activities which can be used.

Chapters 2 and 3 present information about "homemade" equipment which should be readily accessible to children and teachers alike. The equipment presented in chapter 4 is not necessarily inexpensive. However, the equipment is unique and the activity possibilities that become available with its use offer the teacher many excellent ways of meeting physical education objectives.

Chapter 5 offers a discussion of activities created as a result of using the equipment and activities presented in this book. It is the writer's opinion that this discussion will prove valuable to the teacher of elementary school physical education.

Chapter 2

Equipment Made with Throw Away Items and Accompanying Activities

The equipment presented in this chapter is especially noteworthy because it is not necessary to purchase construction materials for it. Most of the materials can be found in the average household.

BLEACH BOTTLE BALL SCOOPS

Materials Needed: ½ gallon plastic bleach bottle.

Construction Instructions:
1. Rinse the bottle thoroughly.
2. Cut out the bottom (see illustration).
3. Tape the bottom rim—overlap the tape both inside and outside the edge of the bottle.

Activities:
1. **Throwing:**   A Whiffle Ball (See appendix for source of purchase) is used with the bleach bottle scoop. You actually "sling" the ball rather than throwing it. The bottle should be moved forward using the forearm rather than the entire arm. With the upper arm held at shoulder height the forearm is extended. The

wrist is snapped as the ball is thrown from the scoop. Note: The ball should roll out of the scoop along the back side somewhat as a ball is slung in the game of jai-alai (see illustration).

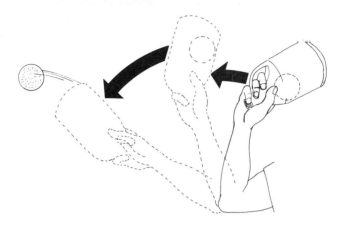

2. **Catching:**   The ball is caught by moving the scoop in front of the oncoming ball. The ball is allowed to land in the open end of the scoop.
3. **Scoop and Throw:**   The playing area is divided in half by a middle line. Each of two teams is assigned one half of the playing area. Whiffle balls are lined up on the middle line between the two teams. On the whistle, players run to the middle, scoop up the balls and throw them into the opponent's territory. Players must remain in their own half of the playing area. As balls are thrown into a player's territory, they are caught and thrown back in to the opponent's territory. After a period of time the referee blows the whistle and all play stops. The number of balls on each side of the middle line are counted. The team with the least number of balls on their side of the line scores a point. Repeat until one team has scored 5 points. The more balls that are used the greater the amount of catching and throwing.
4. **Whiffle End Ball:**   Details are available in: Charles B. Corbin, *Becoming Physically Educated in the Elementary School.* (Philadelphia: Lea and Febiger, 1969), p. 267.

Teaching Suggestions:
1. Scoops can also be made by cutting down the front of the bottle lower than the back as in a flour or sugar scoop. Such a scoop allows greater throwing force to be applied to the ball.

2. Different companies make bottles in various colors. If team-type games were developed, each team could have bottles distinctive in color from those of other teams.
3. Modifications of Newcomb, basketball and softball can be developed using the scoops.

NYLON STOCKING RACKETS

Materials Needed: Coat hanger, nylon stocking, tape, string or wire.

Construction Instructions:

1. Bend coat hanger into diamond shape (see illustration). Note: Circular and rectangular rackets can be made also.
2. Straighten hanger hook.
3. Insert hanger into stocking, pushing end of hanger into toe of stocking.
4. Pull stocking tight around hanger.
5. Tape or tie stocking to the hanger just above the handle.
6. Tape the handle.
7. For greater strength, two hangers can be used.
8. The stocking may be taped to the hanger (around the edge) for greater strength.

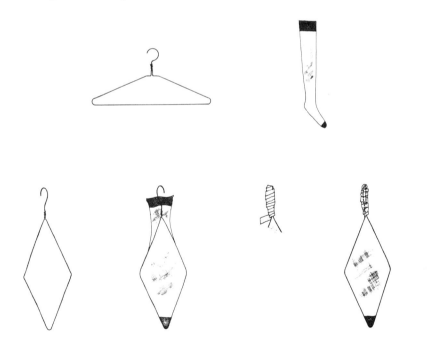

Activities:

1. **Badminton:**   Use the racket with a badminton bird for all modifications of the game. Basic skills can be learned by hitting a bird over a net, over a rope, or just by volleying back and forth.
2. **Puff Ball or Yarn Ball Badminton:**   All forms of badminton can be played using a puff ball.
3. **Ball Balance Relay:**   The stocking racket is also useful for balancing relays. One type requires students to balance a rubber ball on the face of the racket while running.

YARN BALLS

Materials Needed: Yarn, cardboard, string or wire.

Construction Instructions:

1. Cut two large cardboard light weight circles about 3 to 4 inches in diameter. Cut a hole 1½ to 2 inches in diameter in the center of the cardboard circles.
2. Place the circles together one on top of the other. Wrap yarn around the two circles until the holes are nearly full.
3. Cut the yarn around the outside edge of the 4-inch circle. Slide the two circles apart and tie the yarn in the center with string or with wire. Make sure the string is tied *tight*.
4. Cut away the cardboard circles and fluff the ball until it is round.

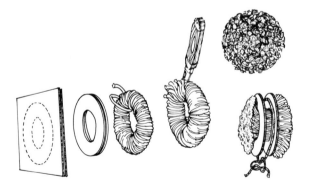

Activities:

1. The balls are excellent for use with nylon stocking rackets.
2. The balls may be used in a manner similar to balls or bean bags for fundamental skill learning or movement exploration.

BICYCLE INNER TUBE

Materials Needed: Old bicycle inner tubes of various sizes.

Construction Instructions:
1. Check the inner tubes to see that they are not torn.
2. Wash the inner tube.
3. Wrap a tape strip around inner tubes to denote the amount of strength required to stretch them. Use a different color of tape for tubes that stretch easily. Also use different colors for different sizes of tubes. Children can select an appropriate tube according to tape color.

Strength Exercises:
1. **Curls:**   Loop the tube under the feet (see illustration). With both hands, flex the arms to the shoulder. Lower the hands to the starting position. Repeat.
2. **Upward Rowing:**   Loop the tube under the feet. Let both arms hang in front of the body. Grasp the tube with both hands, palms toward the body. Pull up, keeping elbows out until the tube is touching the chin. Lower to starting position. Repeat.
3. **Military Press:**   Lying on the back with the inner tube under the shoulders and the hands near the shoulders, grasp each end of the tube with the hands (see illustration). Extend the arms up and to the front of the body until they are fully extended. Return to starting position. Repeat.

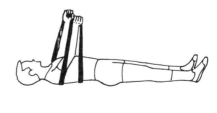

4. **Leg Extension:**   Step inside the tube. Lift the tube until it is just under the arms. Lie down. Lift the feet until the knees are against the chest (see illustration). Hook the feet under the tube. Extend the legs against the resistance of the tube. Return and repeat.

5. **Knee Straightener:**   Stand. Loop the tube over one shoulder. Lift the same side foot up behind the body and hook it in the tube. Straighten the leg against the tube by extending the knee. Return and repeat. Do this exercise with each leg.

Teaching Suggestions:

1. Many other exercises and variations are possible. Allow children to develop their own exercises under your supervision.
2. Some excellent exercises can be developed when children work with *partners.*
3. Tubes can be looped around a pole or rail for developing exercises. This allows many different variations.
4. For some exercises the tube may be *doubled* to offer more resistance.
5. If the tube offers too little resistance it may be necessary to do exercises with one arm or one leg at a time.
6. If tubes break they may be tied back together and reevaluated as to resistance and size.
7. Children like to develop exercise routines to music.

INNER TUBE RELAYS AND GAMES:[1]

1. **Through the Tube Relay:**   On "Go" the first student in each line runs to a designated line where inner tubes of equal size are located. When the runner reaches the line he performs the task

1. Credit is given David E. Corbin, who developed these activities.

and then runs back and touches the next person in line. This continues until all persons in each line have completed the tasks. In this relay, place the inner tube on one leg and up and over the body and head until it comes off the other leg.

2. **Over the Top Relay:** The relay is performed the same as number 1 except that the runner passes the inner tube over the head and body and leaves it on the floor. (The relay can be done with two or three students at a time).

3. **Step Through Relay:** The relay is performed the same as number 1 except the runner passes the inner tube over the feet and pulls it up over the body and the head.

4. **Over the Chair Relay:** The relay is performed the same as number 1 except that the runner passes the tube over his head and body and *chair* while sitting in the chair.

In the above relays a row of several tubes (five to seven) can be placed in front of each team. Each person then would have to do the task with each tube before returning to touch the next person.

In the next set of relays the students have the tubes at the beginning of each line. They do the specific task continuously while moving to a line and back. The tube is then handed to the next person or persons in line.

5. **Three Leg Relay:** One side of a tube circles one leg of each of two people. Both run without letting the legs come out of the tube.

6. **Leg Tie Relay:** Double tube over and place it over both feet of one person (below the knees), who must run to line and back without losing tube.

7. **Two Man Hop Relay:** Two people with both feet in tube (tube below knees). They hop together down and back.

8. **Two Together Relay:** Two people with tube around waists run to line and back. Give tube to next two persons in line.

9. **Chariot Relay:** First person with tube around waist, second person holding tube from behind (horse and carriage style). They run to line and change, second person putting tube around him and first person now running behind holding tube.

10. **One Foot Hop Relay:** Hook tube over foot behind the back and hold the end of the tube over the shoulder. Hop on one foot to line and back.

11. **Two Tube Relay:** One tube under each foot with the other end of the tubes held one in each hand. Run down and back without losing tube from either foot.

Games:
1. Tag can be played with players performing various tasks with tubes. See tasks numbers 5-11 above.
2. Put ten persons on a team. Give each team one large inner tube. On command each team tries to get all players into the tube at waist level.
3. Divide students into sets of two. The students of each set are placed back to back with the tube around their waists, facing lines that have been drawn in front of each. On command each tries to pull his opponent over the line.
4. Tie several tubes together and form a team, having as many students on the team as you have tubes tied together. Team must run to line—each player then getting in one of the tubes. The entire team runs back across the line while in the joined tubes.

Teaching Suggestions:

For relays and games the valve stems should be cut off the inner tubes.

INNER TUBE STRIPS

Materials Needed: Old automobile inner tube.

Construction Instructions:
1. Cut strips approximately 1½ inches in width.
2. Make sure to cut straight and not at an angle. There will be some waste if strips are to be cut straight for even stretch (see illustration).

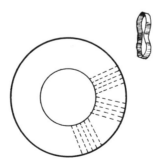

Activities:
1. The activities are the same as for the bicycle tubes except that they must be adapted because of shorter length and different resistance.

BROOMSTICKS

Materials Needed: Old brooms or mops.

Construction Instructions:

1. Cut off the broom stick so that as much of the stick as possible can be used (see illustration).

Activities:[2]

1. **Horse Racing:** Place the broomstick between the legs while holding one end with one hand. The other end drags on the ground. The stick is the horse. Different types of races can be conducted.

2. **Broomstick Hockey:** Divide the group into two teams on a hard surface court, with lines of equal length at either end to serve as goal lines. A rubber quoit or similar type ring is used as a puck to be propelled with the end of the broomstick over the goal line for a score. As skills improve the goals should be made narrower.

3. **Broomstick Roll-Off:** Place five or more broomsticks on the floor with one student standing on them. Another student steps on the sticks and tries to roll and slide back and forth with his feet so that the first student loses his balance and falls off the sticks. (This can be done with two to four students per group of sticks.)

4. **Jump Sticks:** Place the broomsticks on the floor about two feet apart in any formation (circle, line, etc.). As in hop-scotch, have the students hop between the sticks (one or more students at a

2. From David E. Corbin, "The Magic of Broomsticks," *The Physical Educator* 27 (1970): 87-88. Used by permission.

time) varying the design of sticks and also the foot that the student hops with.

5. **Stick Balance:** Have the students balance sticks perpendicular to the floor on the palm of their hand. Vary the balance points as skill progresses (foot, fingers, elbow).

6. **Stick Toss:** With the stick balanced on the palm or fingers try to toss stick to another student without losing the balance of the stick (i.e. palm to palm without holding the stick—it must be balanced). Count successful successive attempts.

7. **Stick Throw:** Line students up facing same direction; on signal throw the stick like a spear. Then all students retrieve and face other direction. Make sure they throw on command only.

8. **Broombatives:**
   A. Each student holds a stick and crosses stick of another student. As they hold the stick with both hands they try to push their opponent across a line that is drawn behind each student (about three feet).
   B. Two students face each other and hold a broomstick. Each student tries to touch the right (his right) end of the stick to the ground. Whoever touches his end to the ground is the winner.

9. **Tuck Jump:** Each student holds a stick in both hands and tries to jump through the arms and over the stick by tucking the knees to the chest, without releasing the grip on the stick.

10. **Over the Head:** Start with a wide grip on the stick with both hands. With straight arms take the stick over head and down to the back. See how close the students can get their hands and still do the trick with straight arms.

11. **Twister:** With two to ten students having one stick end in each hand, form a circle (student-stick-student-stick, etc. all the way around). Then one student at a time crawls under, steps over, or jumps over (with one or two legs) any of the other broomsticks. Those who let go of any stick must go start another circle. The last one to let go in the circle is the champ.

12. **Back Scratcher:**[3] Hold a broomstick with the palms facing away from the body and the arms crossed over one another. Bend the elbows so that the wand can go over and behind the head. Try to pass the broomstick down the length of the body all the way to the heels. Then step over the stick so that the stick is in

---

3. Credit is given David E. Corbin who developed activities nos. 12-23.

front of the body again. Do not release the grip on the stick any time throughout the stunt.

13. **Contortion:** Hold a stick (4 feet in length) with both hands, palms facing away from the body. Step through the stick with both legs (one at a time). Bring the stick over the head. Step around one arm with the leg on the same side. Place the leg that went around the arm inside the stick (between you and the stick). Pull on the stick until it is all the way over the back and head. Then step over the stick until you are back to the original position that you started in. Be certain not to let go of the stick during any part of the stunt.

14. **Twist Under:** Hold a stick upright by grasping the top of the stick so that the other end of the stick is on the floor. Twist so that you pass under the arm holding the stick without letting go of the stick, taking it off the floor, or touching knee to the floor. Do it with the other arm, too.

15. **Jig Saw:** Two students face each other both holding on to one stick with both hands. They lean back and sit down slowly while they swing their hips from side to side as they sit down. The same stunt can be performed in the opposite direction.

16. **Wand Whirl:** Stand a wand upright in front of you holding it at the top so that the other end touches the floor. Release your grasp and quickly turn around (360°) and catch the wand before it touches the floor. Do it in both directions. Then try it making two full turns.

17. **Thread the Needle:** While standing in a pike position with the wand held in front of the body with both hands, bend the knees so that the legs pass between the arms and over the wand. Return to the original position without touching back or feet to the floor and without touching the feet to the wand.

18 **Wand Catch:** Stand a wand on one end and hold it up with the index finger. Bring the foot quickly over the stick, letting it go and catching it again with the finger before it falls. Do the stunt with the right and left leg both to the inside of the stick and from the inside out. Short students may have to stand on a bench or platform to perform this stunt.

19. **Stick Wrestle:** Two students face each other holding a stick between them. The stick should be gripped so that the student's hands are alternately placed. (Neither student has both hands gripped inside or outside the other student's.) On command each student tries to make the other student let go of the stick by twisting the stick back and forth and applying pressure.

20. **Tug-O-War:**   Using a stick instead of a rope, students can have a tug-o-war in one of several ways:
    A.   Two students face each other and pull in opposite directions until one student pulls the other across a line drawn on the ground between them.
    B.   Same as A except each student holds two sticks (one end of each stick in each hand).
    C.   Same as A except student may pull using only one hand.
    D.   Students face in opposite directions holding the ends of two sticks (one end in each hand). Each tries to pull the other over the line.

21. **Ring the Wand:**   This game requires two teams (five to seven players on each team). Each team has one or two goals. Goals are persons who stand on a chair at the end of the court (out of bounds at end of a basketball court) and hold a wand in their hands. The object of the game is to throw a deck tennis ring or quoit around the wand being held by the goal. The players may not run when the ring is in their possession. Fouling rules are the same as basketball and boundaries are the same. The game is started with a center jump. If the goalie does step off the chair to catch the ring no point is scored and the other team throws the ring in bounds.

22. **Chariot Race:**   This requires a gym-type floor. One student sits on the floor holding one end of two sticks in each hand. Another student holds the other ends of the sticks and faces the same direction (he is standing). On command the standing student pulls the other student to a designated line and back while the sitting student merely slides along on the floor behind the student pulling him. This can be done in relay formation or simply as a race.

23. **Limbo:**   This is the West Indian dance in which a student faces a stick that is held or supported on each end. The performing student bends backward and passes under the stick without touching the hands to the floor. See how low you can go. It is best performed to special limbo music, but any music in fast tempo will suffice. The most successful performers will find that the feet should form a wide base and the knees be close together. The angle of the upper and lower leg is approximately 90°.

Teaching Suggestions:

1.   The maturity and skill achievement level of each child will best determine for which ones of the foregoing "Broomstick" activi-

ties the individual child is best suited. Safety measures, including prerequisite skill instruction and "spotting" where appropriate, should be considered before children participate in the activities presented above.

2. Several substitutes can be used instead of broomsticks if broomsticks are not available. Plastic golf tubes, used to hold golf clubs in a golf bag, are sold at most sporting good stores at low cost. Bamboo poles cut in short lengths can be used. Finally the cardboard cylinders on which wrapping paper is rolled can serve as broomsticks. They are, however, easily damaged.

CHINESE JUMP ROPE[4]

Materials Needed: Elastic cord (¼ inch) or elastic strips (⅜- or ½-inch width).

Construction Instructions:
1. Cut elastic in six to eight foot lengths.
2. Tie the two ends of the cord together to make an elastic loop.

Activities:

Chinese jump rope consists of several stunts to be performed, one at a time, by each child. The child performs the stunts in the order listed below until he cannot complete the next stunt. The next child then jumps until he misses.

To start the activity two children stand inside the elastic strip with the elastic looped around their ankles. Their feet should be together with approximately three feet between children.

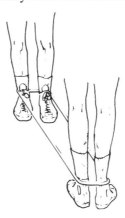

4. Thanks to Joyce Takacs for her assistance in outlining this activity.

The stunts to be performed are:

1. **Toe Hooks:**   Stand with both feet on the same side of the two elastic strips. Step over the nearest elastic strip with the near foot and tap the toe between the strips. Return to starting position. Now a step over the far elastic strip catching the near strip over your ankle. Tap the toe on the ground. Return to starting position. Repeat each of the above steps three times alternating one skill then the other. Next step to the other side of the strips and repeat.

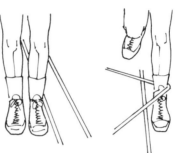

2. **Ankle Tangle:**   Stand with feet straddling the two elastic strips. Jump in the air, cross the legs and land with the opposite foot outside the elastic strips (the legs are crossed). Still facing the same direction, shift the feet by uncrossing the legs. *DO NOT* let the strips slip off the ankles. Both strips should now be behind one ankle and in front of the other. Jump in the air allowing the strips to slip off the ankles. Land straddling the two strips (one foot on each side).

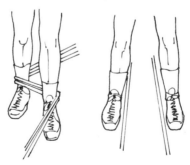

3. **Boxes:**   Stand with both feet on the same side of the two elastic strips. Step over the far strip catching the near side strip on the ankle. Place the foot on the ground outside the far strip. Step over the near strip with the other foot and form a "BOX" with the feet located in each corner. Jump in the air allowing the

strips to slip off the ankles. Stand straddling the two strips (one foot on each side).

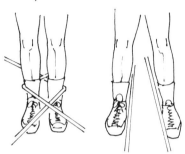

4. **Triangles**: Start just as in "Boxes" but step into the triangle with the second foot so that both feet are at the top of the triangle. Jump in the air allowing the strips to slip off the ankles. Land straddling the two strips (one on each side).

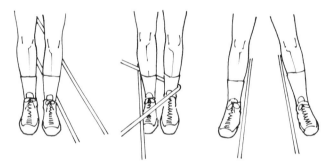

5. **Triangle Shuffle**: Do a triangle (as above). Instead of jumping out of the strips, jump across into the other elastic strip forming another triangle, this time with the opposite strip as the top of the triangle. Now jump in the air allowing the strips to slide off the ankles (one on each side).

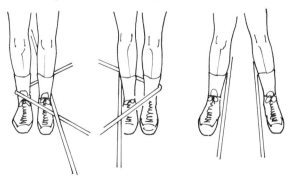

6. **Double Toe Hooks:** Stand facing both elastic strips. Jump over the far strip catching the near strip over both toes. Land outside the far strip with the elastic forming a "Triangle." Jump in the air allowing the strip to slip off the ankle. Land with both feet outside the strips with the heels near the strip opposite the place you began. Repeat facing the other direction.

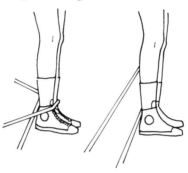

7. **Double Triangles:** Stand facing both elastic strips. With one foot, step over the far elastic strip catching the toe under the near strip. Place the foot on the ground. Now step forward with the other foot catching the toe under the other elastic strip and step over the first strip. Both ankles should now be enclosed by small triangles. Jump in the air allowing the strips to slip off the ankles. Land with both feet on the side of the strips opposite the beginning position.

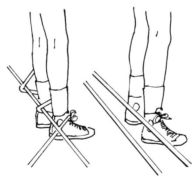

Teaching Suggestions:

1. Children may wish to raise the elastic to knee level or hip level once skills have been mastered at ankle level.
2. Slight modifications of skills especially the "ankle tangle" and "double toe hooks" may be necessary as the height of the elastic strip is raised. Let the children develop their own modifications.

3. Stakes may be used to hold the Chinese Jump Rope to allow more children to be active.
4. Very young children can accomplish the skills if they are allowed to hold on (to another child, etc.) as they perform the skills.
5. Skills are most easily performed without shoes.
6. Some excellent continuous rhythmical patterns and foot movements can be developed to music using the Chinese Jump Rope. Many of the tinikling steps (see page 35-39) may be modified for use with this activity. Allow children to develop their own skill modifications to music.

WRAPPED NEWSPAPER BALLS[5]

Materials Needed: Old newspapers and masking tape (other types of soft tape will work).

Construction Instructions:
1. Crumple several sheets of newspaper into a ball. Compress to the desired size.
2. Tape around the ball in a crisscross manner until the outer edges of the paper are fully taped.
3. Mold the shape of the ball with the hands. Draw the tape firmly against high edges.

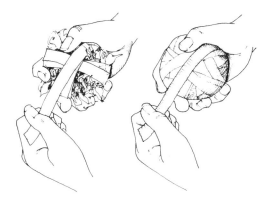

Activities:
1. The newspaper balls can be used for any activity which does not require of them considerable bounce, or contact (for example: being hit with a bat).

---

5. Credit is given to Paul Shimon who assisted in the development of this idea.

2. The balls are inexpensive—each child can have his own. The balls are excellent for fundamental skill instruction.
3. These balls work very well when used with Bleach Bottle Scoops.

TIN CAN STILTS

Materials Needed: Two one-pound coffee cans and heavy string or cord.

Construction Instructions:
1. With a nail or a metal punch, make holes on either side and near the bottom of each coffee can.
2. Insert the cord from the outside of the can through the holes on each side.
3. Tie the cord so that the knot stays inside the can. The loop outside the can should be long enough to enable a child standing on the cans to hold the cord loops at about waist height.
4. Leave the plastic lids on the cans to prevent slippage, to prevent floor damage, and to prevent the cans from bending.

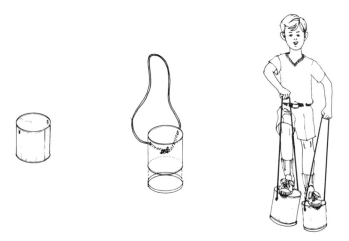

Activities:
1. The child stands on the cans, one under each foot, while grasping the cords in each hand. Holding the can tightly to the feet, the child walks on the cans using them as stilts.
2. Coffee can stilts can be used as a relay activity.
3. Stilts work well as an activity for use on an obstacle course.

LID FLYING SAUCERS

Materials Needed: Plastic lids from one- and two-pound coffee cans.

Construction Instructions:

1. Lids are merely removed from coffee cans and are ready for use.
2. Different color lids can be collected for a variety of uses.

Activities:

1. Sail the flying saucer in the same manner that a "FRISBEE" is tossed.
2. **Fly Away:** Use many saucers and play the game as you play "Scoop and Throw" on page 4. Throw saucers instead of balls.
3. **Target Shooting:** Children try to sail saucers at a predetermined target.

COFFEE CAN TARGETS

Materials Needed: Coffee cans, string, and boards.

Construction Instructions:

1. Arrange cans on a board in a way that would make them good targets in a target throwing game (see illustration). Trace a circle to outline the desired location where the can will be fixed to the board.
2. Drill quarter-inch holes in the board where the cans are to be fixed to the board. The holes should be about two inches apart.
3. Punch two holes in the bottom of each can with a nail or metal punch. Holes should be about two inches apart.
4. Loop a string through one hole in the board, up through one hole in the can, down through the other hole in the can and out

through the second hole in the board. Secure the can to the board by taping the string tightly on the back side of the board.
5. Tie on all cans using this same arrangement.

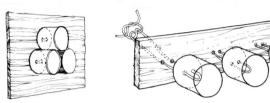

Activities:

1. Coffee can targets are excellent for use with bean bags and wrapped newspaper balls.
2. Coffee can targets can be used for "Washers" (see page 30) especially for younger children.

TIRES

Materials Needed: Old rubber tire carcasses.
Construction Instructions:
1. Wash the tires.

Activities:

1. **Roll the Tire:**   Children run or walk along side a tire as they roll it over a prescribed course.

2. **Bounce on the Tire:**   With the tire on its side, the child places one foot on each edge of the tire straddling the hole. He jumps up and down using the tire as a spring board. This is a good activity for inclusion in an obstacle course or a circuit.

3. **Rubber Tire Markers:**   Tires can be buried so that one half of the tire is exposed. The exposed part of the tire can be used as boundary markers for soccer and other games.

MILK CARTONS

Materials Needed: One gallon or half-gallon cardboard milk containers.

Construction Instructions:
1. Wash the insides of the containers and make sure they do not contain any milk or water.
2. In some cases it is desirable to stuff them with old newspapers.

Activities:
1. **Milk Carton Soccer:**   The game is played like regular soccer except that a milk carton is used for the ball.

2. **Kicking Relays and Drills:**   Relays and drills used in the teaching of soccer can be worked on using a milk carton instead of a ball.
3. **Crab Soccer:**   Soccer played while performing the crab walk works quite well with a milk carton used as a ball.
4. **Milk Carton Bowling Pins:**   Milk cartons can be used as pins in bowling games as well as for markers in relays, etc.

Chapter 3

Low Cost Equipment and Accompanying Activities

While the play equipment presented in this chapter does require an initial expenditure of a moderate amount, the expense is minimal compared to that usually required to supply one piece of equipment for each child. What is more, these homemade items are quite flexible in their use.

WOOD BLOCKS

Materials Needed: Wood two or four inches thick.

Construction Instructions:
1. Cut the wood in two inch or four inch squares.
2. Sand the blocks to eliminate splinters and rough edges.
3. In some cases it is desirable to round the corners of the blocks with sand paper.

Activities:
1. **Block Bowling:** A block bowling diagram (see illustration) is outlined on the floor with tape or chalk. Four to six children bowl on each "alley." Children roll two blocks each along the ground attempting to score by landing their block in the block bowling diagram. Two- or four-inch blocks can be used. Scoring is done

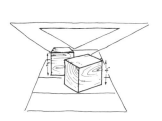
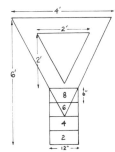

on a regular bowling score sheet. If the first block rolled lands in the area marked "strike," a strike is recorded on the score sheet. If the first block lands in "spare," a spare is recorded. If the first block lands anywhere else it is scored as marked. Those not scoring a strike or a spare with the first block, roll two blocks and count the best of the two. It is suggested that children work in pairs, one bowling and the other retrieving the blocks. Then they reverse roles. The bowler retrieves—the retriever bowls.

2.   **Hop Kick Golf:**[6]   Mark off an 18-hole course as indicated in the illustration. Boxes (holes) should be one foot square and the arrow extending from each box should point in the direction of the next hole. Divide the children so that two or three are starting at each hole at the same time. When the game begins, each child stands on one foot with the other foot held in the air. With his free foot, he kicks his block as many times as is necessary to get it in the next hole. (Follow the arrow). When the block is in the square it is considered in the hole. The children count the number of kicks required to get their block in each hole. A 2-stroke penalty is assessed for touching the ground with the nonkicking foot. Continue play until each child has played every hole.

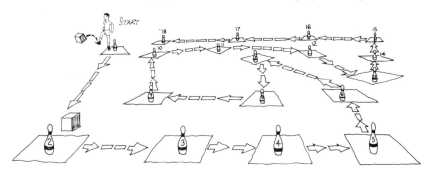

Teaching Suggestions:

1.   Have the children make their own score cards for use in scoring.
2.   For the less skilled children require the block only to enter the square to be in the hole. For the more skilled, make the block hit a bowling pin placed in each square.
3.   As children become more skilled encourage them to hop and kick with the same foot.
4.   **Hop Scotch:**   Wood blocks work well in hop scotch.

6. Adapted from Charles B. Corbin, *Becoming Physically Educated in the Elementary School* (Philadelphia: Lea and Febiger, 1970), p. 278. By permission of the publisher.

LUMEY STICKS

Materials Needed: ½- to ¾-inch dowel rods, broomsticks or ½- to ¾-inch square strips of wood.

Construction Instructions:
1. Cut dowels or wood strips in lengths of six to ten inches.
2. Sticks may be painted if desired. This may be done as a class project in art or some other area.

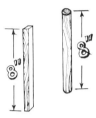

Activities:

Two children, each holding two sticks, sit facing each other. The children sit 2½ to 3 feet apart. The skills listed below are performed to the 1-2-3 rhythm of the music.

THE LUMEY STICK SONG

Children perform the simplest skills first, progressing to the more complex. Skills are listed in order of relative difficulty.

    A. **Stick Hit:** (Three counts performed eight times)
        1. Hit ends of sticks on the floor (down)
        2. Hit sticks together
        3. Hit sticks against sticks of partner
    B. **One Hand Hits:** (Six counts performed four times)
        1. Down
        2. Together
        3. Hit stick in right hand against stick in partner's right hand
        4. Down
        5. Together
        6. Hit stick in left hand against stick in partner's left hand

C. **Cross Toss:**   (Four counts performed six times)
   1. Down
   2. Together
   3. Exchange right hand sticks with partner (toss)
   4. Exchange left hand sticks with partner (toss)

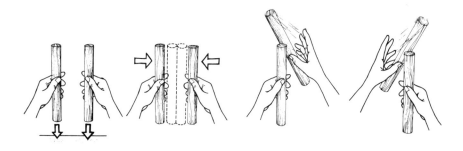

D. **Double Toss:**   (Three counts performed eight times)
   1. Down
   2. Together
   3. Exchange both sticks with partner—one throw wide one narrow

E. **Stick Flip:**   (Six counts performed four times)
   1. Hit the top end of the sticks on the floor (top)
   2. Flip the sticks one revolution in the air (flip)
   3. Down
   4. Together
   5. Toss (right)
   6. Toss (left)

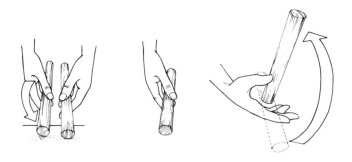

F. **Side Hits:**   (Six counts performed four times)
   1. Down

2. Hit top of sticks to the floor outside the legs
3. Down
4. Together
5. Toss (right)
6. Toss (left)

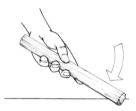

G. **Opposite Side Hits:** (Six counts performed four times)
1. Down
2. Hit tops of sticks to floor reaching to the side over opposite leg (cross arms)
3. Down
4. Together
5. Toss (right)
6. Toss (left)

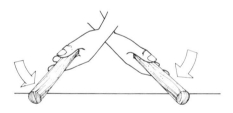

Teaching Suggestions:
1. Any combination of the above skills can be made as long as the total number of counts equals twenty-four.
2. For the initial stages of learning the record **Lummi Sticks** is a valuable teaching aid. The record is available from the Twinson Company (see appendix).
3. More detailed information is available in an article: Joy Garrison and Milly Doren, "Lumey Sticks," *Journal of Health, Physical Education and Recreation.* 27 (March 1956): 19.

WASHERS

Materials Needed: Washers 1½ to 2 inches in diameter, and tin cans.

Construction Instructions:
1. Eight washers are needed for each group of four players. Four washers should be painted with finger nail polish for identification purposes.
2. Two cans should be placed in the ground from ten to twenty feet apart. The size of the opening in the can should vary with the skill ability of the children. The top edge of the can should be at ground level.

Activities:
1. Players are grouped in two teams of two players each.
2. Two players, one from each team, stand at each end of the playing area next to one of the cans.
3. The game is played in much the same way as horseshoes with players pitching the washers attempting to "get them in" the cans.
4. Each player pitches four washers per turn. Players from the last team to score a point pitch first.
5. Washers pitched in the can count three points. Otherwise, the washers nearest the can count one point each. A game is twenty-one points.

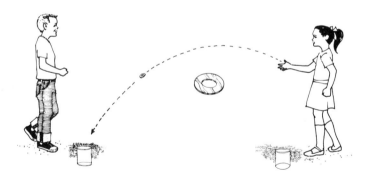

Teaching Suggestions:
1. Vary the distance between cans according to the ability of children.
2. Children may choose to play singles, that is, one against one.

SPONGE RUBBER BALLS

Materials Needed: Pieces of sponge from six to twelve inches thick.

Construction Instructions:
1. Cut sponge in cubes of equal dimensions (6"x6"x6" to 12"x12"x 12").
2. With a sharp knife, trim off the eight corners of the ball (see illustration).

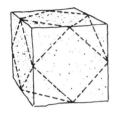 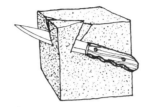 

Activities:
1. **Throwing and Catching:**   These balls are excellent for use with young children because they "give" when they hit a child. The balls react much as a normal ball and can be used indoors.
2. **Soccer Activities:**   These balls have been used quite effectively as indoor soccer balls. They react much as a regular ball though with a slower flight and roll.

BALLOONS

Materials Needed: Balloons of various sizes.

Construction Instructions:
1. Inflate the balloons to slightly less than the normal amount of pressure.
2. Tie off the inflation stem.

Activities:
1. **Volleyball:**   Balloons are excellent for use as volleyballs during the early stages of learning. The slow descent of the balloon makes it easy to teach.
2. **Movement Exploration:**   The movement problems which can be solved by children using balloons are unlimited. Throwing, catching, batting, and volleying are just a few of the skills which can be explored.

Teaching Suggestions:

1. When children master skills with a normal balloon, insert a penny or a similar object inside the balloon. This extra weight causes a faster flight and descent.
2. Have children explore with more than one balloon at a time.

BEACHBALLS

Materials Needed: Beachballs of any size.

Construction Instructions:

1. Inflate.

Activities:

1. **Catching and Throwing:** Beachballs are perhaps the best type of ball available for teaching throwing and catching. Because the balls are large and have a slow flight, they are easily caught by young children. Because they are soft they do not scare children.
2. **Games and Exploration:** Any ball activity can be adapted to the use of beachballs, which are frequently more appropriate than basketballs, volleyballs or playground balls.

PAPER STRIPS

Materials Needed: String, crepe paper, stapling device, and small blocks of wood.

Construction Instructions:

1. Cut crepe paper, or some other type of non-tear paper, into strips two to three inches wide.
2. Cut small blocks of wood to the width of the paper but only a fraction of an inch thick (example: 3" x ¼" x ¼").
3. Staple crepe paper to the wood strip, after folding the edge of the paper over several times to keep it from tearing loose from the strip.
4. Staple the string to the center of the wood strip.

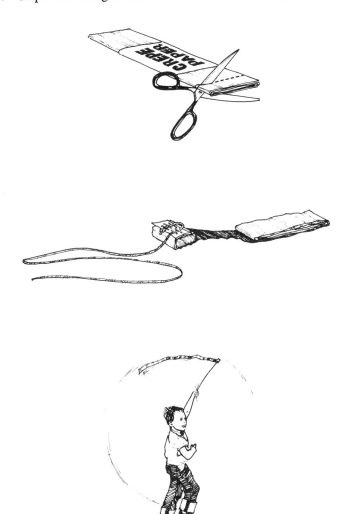

Activities:

1. **Circles:** The child grasps the end of the string furthest from the wood strip. With a waving motion of the arm the wood block and paper strip are swung in a circle over the head or to the side of the body.
2. **Exploration:** Many other patterns are possible, such as a figure 8, and narrow circles. Patterns can also be made while running or performing other locomotor movements.
3. **Relays:** Relays requiring children to perform circle movement while running or hopping are also practical.

HOOPS

Materials Needed: ½- to ¾-inch flexible plastic tubing (available at most hardware stores), dowel rods (sized to fit internal diameter of tubing), and staples.

Construction Instructions:

1. Cut tubing in lengths according to desired size of hoop, normally six to eight feet.
2. Insert a two- to three-inch dowel rod in the flexible plastic tubing at both ends, thus forming a circle or hoop.
3. Staple both ends of the tubing to the dowel rods.

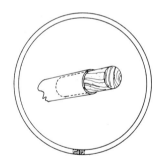

Activities:

1. **Hula Hoops:** Use as regular hula hoop.
2. **Arm and Leg Circles:** Smaller hoops can be made for arm and leg circles. The child swings the arm or leg allowing the hoop to circle. Children may attempt to perform with several hoops at a time.
3. **Jump the Hoop:** Performed like jump rope except that the hoop is used instead of the rope. The hoop is grasped on one

side with both hands placed together. The hands allow the hoop edge to turn inside them as the hoop passes alternately over the head and under the feet.

4. **Roll the Hoop:** Children merely roll the hoop along the ground in a predetermined path.

5. **Run Through the Hoop:** While the hoop is rolling the children can run in and out of the circular opening. Very large hoops can be constructed especially for this activity.

6. **Exploration With Hoops:** Children can explore with the hoops. Such things as spinning, and throwing are possible. Also the hoops may be used to define specific movement spaces to be explored.

BAMBOO POLES

Materials Needed: Bamboo poles.

Construction Instructions:

1. Cut poles in four to ten foot lengths depending on activity to be performed.

2. Note: Bamboo poles are frequently available from carpet stores, as poles are used in storing carpet.

Activities:

1. Any of the activities listed for broomsticks (pages 11-15) can be performed, using short bamboo poles.

2. **Bamboo Pole Dance (Tinikling):** Four children work together using two poles. Two children move the poles while the other two hop in and out of the poles (see illustration). Poles are hit to the ground to a 1-2-3 rhythm. On "one" the poles are hit to the floor, on "two" the poles are again hit against the floor, and on "three' the poles are lifted two to three inches off the ground and are hit together. This 1-2-3 sequence is repeated for the duration of the activity. The two dancers hop in and out of the moving bamboo poles using the following hopping steps:

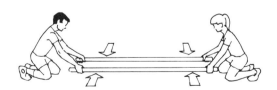

A. *Basic Step*: Stand with side toward poles with both feet outside the poles. On the count "one" step between the poles with the nearest foot. Take the entire body weight on this foot. On "two" shift the weight and hop on the other foot staying inside the two poles. On "three" step out the opposite side on your first foot. Repeat the sequence starting on the count "one" stepping in with the nearest foot (it will be the opposite of the starting foot).

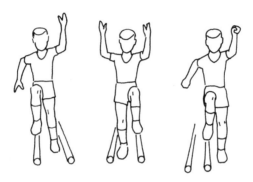

B. *Straddle Step*: Stand with feet straddling the two poles. On "one" hop in between the two poles on both feet. On "two" repeat the two foot hop. On "three" straddle the poles. Repeat keeping the 1-2-3 rhythm.

C. *Turn Step*: On "one" step in between the poles with the near foot. On "two" hop in the air on the same foot and make a half turn landing faced the opposite direction. On "three" step out on the other foot. Repeat, always entering on the same foot.

D. *Cross Step*: For this step a three count starter step is required. On "one" step in between the poles with the near foot. On "two" hop again on the same foot. On "three" step across and out the opposite side of the poles with the other foot.

On "one" of the second measure step back in with your original starting foot. On "two" shift to other foot. On "three" step across and out with your starting foot. Repeat with the 1-2-3 rhythm.

Teaching Suggestions:

1. Many variations are possible including multiple pole dances. Complete details are available in: Charles B. Corbin, *Becoming Physically Educated in the Elementary School* (Philadelphia: Lea and Febiger, 1970), pp. 323-28.

2. The Bamboo Pole Dance can be performed to music. Recommended are "TINIKLING," RCA LPM 1619 (see appendix for address of RCA Victor), and any current records with a three-count rhythm.

3. A complete Bamboo Pole Dance Kit is available from Educational Activities, Inc. (see appendix).
4. Poles are available from Charles H. Demarest Company (see appendix).

BEAN BAGS

Materials Needed: Heavy cloth, sewing machine, measuring cup, and dry beans, peas, or corn.

Construction Instructions:
1. Cut heavy cloth into rectangular pieces of approximately 5" x 10" or 7" x 14". Fold cloth to make 5" x 5" or 7" x 7" squares with the rough side of the cloth exposed.
2. With a sewing machine sew two side folds of the cloth closed. Then turn square pocket inside out exposing the smooth side of the material.
3. Through the open or unsewn side of the square pocket or bag, pour dry beans, peas or corn (one-half cup for small bags and one cup for large bags).
4. Use a sewing machine to sew the opening in the bag closed.

Activities:

1. **Throwing and Catching:** Simple throwing and catching can be performed with bean bags. The bags don't bounce, and because they can be caught by the child's "grabbing" almost any part of them, their use practically assures that these activities will be easier for poorly skilled children.

2. **Movement Exploration:** Like other activities in this book, the movement problems which can be solved with bean bags are only limited by the imagination of the students and the teacher.

Teaching Suggestions:

1. Different color bean bags can be made for different games and activities.

2. Different size bags can be constructed to meet the needs of different size children.

3. Many relays and simple games can be created by children using bean bags.

Chapter *4*

Other Unique Equipment
and Activities

The following equipment and accompanying activities do require a fair expenditure for the initial investment. However, the unique nature of the equipment and activities make them interesting and fun, as well as productive for learning. Sources of equipment are detailed in the appendix.

PARACHUTES

Materials Needed: Twenty to thirty foot parachute.

Construction Instructions:
1. Remove from carcass.
2. Cut circular chute from all attached cords.

Activities:

The following stunts are performed by children in groups ranging in size from ten to forty members. Most of the activities can be done gripping the chute with the palms of the hands facing up or down. Also the activities can be done from sitting, kneeling or standing positions.

1. **The Bubble:** Begin with children in a circle around the chute which is spread on the ground. On "go" children simultaneously lift the chute from the ground, extending their arms over their heads. The children step forward one to two steps to allow the chute to make a full bubble.

2. **The Balloon:** Same as the Bubble except the children step forward several steps, closing the bottom of the chute, making a "balloon" with it.

3. **The Tent:** After making the bubble the children pull the chute down over their shoulders and sit down on the inside edge of the chute. This makes a tent with all children inside an air-filled dome.

4. **Fly Away:** Perform bubble. After the chute reaches full bubble, delay slightly and then have all children release the chute. Let the chute "fly away."

5. **Ground Bubble:** Perform bubble. Pull the chute down placing the edge on the ground. Stand on the edge looking over the top of the bubble.

6. **Heads Under:** Perform a bubble. Pull the chute down, children lie down on their backs pulling the chute to their chests. A ground bubble is formed with the heads under the chute.

7. **Small Waves:** Children pull the chute tight holding it at waist height. Raising and lowering the hands alternately, the children shake the chute, causing small waves.

8. **Large Waves:** Performed as small waves but arms are pulled up and down together.

9. **Pop Corn:** Place Whiffle Balls or Yarn Balls on the chute while performing large waves.

In addition to the stunts suggested above, several games can be developed using the parachute.

10. **Ball Bounce:** Place a playground ball on the chute. With half the children on each side of the chute as teammates, the objective is to force the ball off the other team's side of the chute (large waves are used to move the ball).

11. **Under the Chute:** The children number off by fours. As a bubble is formed, a number is called. Children run under the chute changing places with a member of their own team having the same number.

12. **Circle the Chute:** The children run in a circle while holding the edges of the chute. On "change" the children stop and run the opposite direction. This can be done hopping, skipping, etc., instead of, or in addition to running.

Exercises can also be performed using a parachute. Some examples are listed below:

13. **Tug-O-War:** Children are divided into two teams, one on each side of the chute. On "go" each team tries to pull the other across a line marked on the floor.

14. **Horse Pull:** Facing away from the chute with the arms grasping the chute behind the body, the children pull on the chute. All children are pulling away from the center of the chute.

15: **Curls:** With the parachute held by all children—arms down at sides—they lean back and curl the arms up at the elbow. When arms are fully "curled" they are held there for several seconds.

16. **Roll the Chute:** Lay the chute open on the ground. Divide the class into two groups. On "go" each group tries to roll up their half of the chute ahead of the other.

Teaching Suggestions:

1. Many other variations are possible. Complete details are available in the following articles: (1) S. Popen, and F. S. Miller, "Go Parachuting," *Journal of Health, Physical Education and Recreation.* 38 (April 1967): 24-25; and (2) L. J. Johnson, "Parachute Play for Exercise," *Journal of Health, Physical Education and Recreation.* 38 (April 1967): 26-27.

2. A record entitled "Rhythmic Parachute Play" is available from Education Activities, Inc. (see appendix).

3. Parachutes are available from J. A. Preston Company (see appendix).

CARGO NETS

Materials Needed: Cargo nets (see illustration).

Equipment Source: Cargo nets are available from Sterling Recreation Products (see appendix).

Activities:

Several basic exercises and games can be played using the suspended cargo net. A few examples are listed below:

1. **Climb the Net:** Using hands and feet, climb the net. The cargo net allows many children to climb at the same time.

2. **Hand Climb:** Same as above except only the hands are used.

3. **Climbing Relays:** Relays can be performed using the following: up and down the net, over the net, and through a net hole.

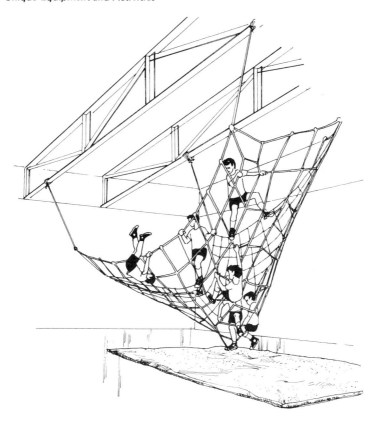

4. **Movement Exploration:** Many movement problems can be posed for children using the cargo net.

Teaching Suggestions:

1. The Cargo Net can be suspended like a basket (see illustration) or by one side for simple climbing.
2. More complete details for activities on the cargo net can be found in the following sources: (1) J. S. Hichwa, "The Cargo Net," *Journal of Health, Physical Education and Recreation.* 41 (January 1970): 30-31; and H. E. Bellardini, "A Sampling of Activities for the Cargo Net," *Journal of Health, Physical Education and Recreation.* 41 (January 1970): 32-33.

TUBE TUMBLING

Materials Needed: A large truck or tractor inner tube and mats.

Construction Instructions:
1. Inflate the tube.
2. Drape a mat over the inflated tube.

Activities:
1. **Hop the Hole:** The child runs toward the tube, jumps on the near side of the hole, springs in the air, and lands on both feet on the mat about one foot beyond the tube (see illustration).

2. **Two Touch Hops:** Performed as above except the child bounces from the front of the tube over the hole to the back of the tube, then he jumps to the mat beyond the tube.
3. **Seat Drop:** The child runs toward the tube, jumps on the near side of the tube, springs in the air, and lands in a sitting position in the hole of the tube.

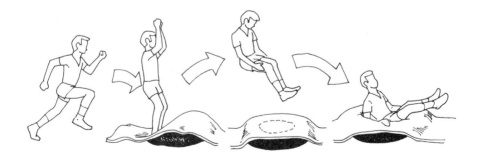

4. **Roll the Hole:** The child runs toward the tube, places both hands on the front of the tube and performs a forward roll over the hole.

Teaching Suggestions:

1. Many other modifications are possible including twists, half twists, handsprings, cartwheels, jack springs and others. More information is available in the following sources: (1) C. B. Corbin, *Becoming Physically Educated in the Elementary School.* (Philadelphia: Lea and Febiger, 1969), pp. 220-24; and (2) G. O'Quinn, *Gymnastics for Elementary School Children.* Dubuque, Iowa: Wm. C. Brown Company Publishers, 1967), pp. 91-100.

CRASH PADS

Materials Needed: Mats of various shape and thickness ranging from six to twenty-four inches.

Equipment Source: Covered crash pads of various shapes and sizes are available from Skill Development Equipment Company (see appendix).

Activities:

1. **Standard Tumbling Activities:** These mats are ideal for such traditional tumbling stunts as forward rolls, backward rolls, handsprings, forward and back aerials, etc. Because of the extra thickness of the mats children can perform stunts without fear of injury.
2. **Learning Tumbling Through Exploration:** Because spotting is *less* necessary with the crash pads and because many creative shapes of mats are available (incline mats, barrel mats, donut mats, etc.) exploration with tumbling is possible. After preliminary instruction, students can work "on their own" with different mats thus creating more activity and more learning.

GYM SCOOTERS

Materials Needed: Gym scooters (small traveling platforms supported on four wheels).

Equipment Source: Titus Gym Scooter Company (see appendix).

Activities:

1. **Relays:**   Relays can be performed using the scooter in each of the following positions: one hand supported on scooter, two hands supported, both knees supported, stomach supported, seat supported, one knee supported. Modifications of the above are possible using two scooters and working with a partner.
2. **Games:**   Modified soccer, basketball, and other games are possible using scooters as the source of locomotion.

Teaching Suggestions:

1. Instruct children in proper skills and safe driving before relays and games are introduced.
2. More complete details for activities using the gym scooter are available in the following sources: (1) R. E. Titus, *Games, Stunts, and Relays for Titus Scooters* (Winfield, Kansas: Titus Co., 1956); and (2) G. Kirchner, *Physical Education for Elementary School Children,* 2d ed. (Dubuque, Iowa: Wm. C. Brown Company Publishers, 1970), pp. 149-51.

Chapter 5

The Use of Movement Routines

In the beginning stages of skill learning it is important that children have the opportunity to "overlearn" skills. In other words, skillful performers are people who have repeated a task so many times that the movement becomes automatic. Unfortunately children get bored with skill drills and are quick to ask "when do we play games" even before the skills necessary for the game are actually learned. For this reason, an important challenge to anyone interested in teaching skills to children is to create activities in which interest is maintained while skills are overlearned or repeated.

The purpose of this chapter is to present information on how "Routines" can be used to promote skill learning. A "Routine" is an original collection of skills created by the student. While the actual skills may be introduced by the teacher, the unique arrangement of the skills in a planned presentation constitutes a routine. In other words children take simple skills, put them in a program of their own, and practice their own program or routine which can later be presented to the other children in the class.

TUMBLING ROUTINES

Tumbling stunts provide an excellent activity area for the development of routines. After the basic skills such as forward rolls, back rolls, cartwheels, log rolls, handsprings, fish flops, shoulder rolls and others are taught, each student creates his own routine. A routine may consist of a specific time period (one or two minutes) or a number of laps down the mats. Whatever the length, the unique combination of skills is the child's. Not only does the child get skill overlearning but he has a feeling of accomplishment associated with his own creation. Other areas in which routines can be developed are discussed in the following section.

47

JUMPNASTICS[7]

Jumpnastics is an activity which combines hopping movements of the feet with simple arm movements. Details for organization and participation follow.

Class Organization

One of the advantages of Jumpnastics is the relatively small play space required for the activity. An area fifty by fifty feet is adequate to accommodate a class of thirty to forty children. The children are divided into squads, such as in performing relays. Each squad can include from two to six children. The fewer the number in each squad, the more activity each squad member receives. However, several children per squad is desirable to allow rest between Jumpnastics "laps" and also fewer squads allows closer supervision by the teacher.

Once the children are grouped in squads the first child performs one Jumpnastics "lap" over the distance of forty to fifty feet. A "lap" refers to the performance of a series or arm maneuvers while hopping across the play area. The children continue until each child in each squad has completed a "lap." Specific Jumpnastics skills include any of a series of arm movements, done in any of several body positions using one of the several basic foot movements or basic steps. The arm movements are performed to the hopping rhythm of the feet. Each "lap" may involve practice of previously learned skills or the introduction and learning of a new Jumpnastics skill.

Once the children have learned the basic Jumpnastics skills, (see illustrations) they may spend some time combining basic skills into personal routines. Performance of routines includes performing a series of laps across the play area which in turn includes a combination of skills selected by the child. Several example routines are suggested. It should be made clear that there is no limit to the number of routines that are possible. It is likely that there will be as many routines as there are children in the group.

7. Adapted from Charles B. Corbin, "Jumpnastics," *The Physical Educator.* 26 (1969): 84-86. Used by permission.

BASIC JUMPNASTIC SKILLS

Foot Movements

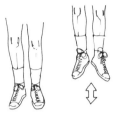

Kangaroo Hop—Do two foot hop across play area.

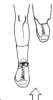

One Foot Hop—Do one foot hop across play area.

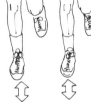

Hot Sidewalk Hop—Hop alternately (two times) one each foot.

Jumping Jack—Hop alternately spreading and returning the feet together.

Hop Kick—Hop on one foot kicking alternately with the other foot.

Arm Movements

Butterfly Swing—Swing the arms alternately from above head to the side at shoulder height.

Jackknife Swing—Swing the arms alternately from above the head to a position in front of the body at shoulder height.

Fan Swing—Swing arms from sides to front (shoulder height).

Pump Swing—Push arms from a position near shoulders to a position in front of the body. Return arms near shoulders.

Punch Swing—Push arms from a position near shoulders to a position to the sides. Return.

Sample Routines

Routine #1: (Simple)	Lap 1—Kangaroo Hop—Jackknife Swing—	
	Lap 2—Kangaroo Hop—Pump Swing—	
	Lap 3—Kangaroo Hop—Punch Swing—	
	Lap 4—Jumping Jack—Butterfly Swing—	
Routine #2:	Lap 1—One Foot Hop—Combined Swing—	
	Lap 2—Kangaroo Hop—Combined Swing— Sideways	
	Lap 3—Jumping Jack—Butterfly Swing— Backward	
	Lap 4—Hot Sidewalk Hop—Butterfly Swing—	
Routine #3: (Difficult)	Lap 1—Hop Kick—Butterfly Swing—	
	Lap 2—Jumping Jack—Punch Swing—Pike— Backward	
	Lap 3—Kangaroo Hop—Combined Swing— Stoop	
	Lap 4—Jumping Jack—Combined Swing.	

Teaching Suggestions:

1. In the beginning the teacher may randomly assign children to squads, and then may move from squad to squad for instructional purposes after initial demonstration. However, after individual differences become apparent, it is desirable to group children homogenously so that the more skillful children can move to advanced skills, and so that the the teacher can work with specific groups of children according to specific needs.

2. As children become sophisticated in Jumpnastics, simple gymnastics skills, such as rolls, and animal walks, may be included in the performance of personal routines.

3. Once basic skills are learned, the children may find it enjoyable to perform Jumpnastics to music. Jumpnastics are easily adapted to rhythm. The performer merely does the basic foot movements to the beat of the music. A complete manual of Jumpnastics and two long play albums are available from Educational Activities, Inc. (see appendix).

4. Jumpnastics skills can be performed backward or to either side, as well as facing forward.

5. Jumpnastics skills can be performed in pike and stoop, as well as in the standing position.

BALL ROUTINES

Materials Needed: One playground or rhythm ball for each child.

Ball Skills: Some of the skills that can be included in a ball routine are as follows: one hand bounce, two hand bounce, one hand bounce alternating hands, throw and catch, bounce pass, two hand pass, one hand pass, high toss, roll the ball. Any or all of these skills, plus others created by the children, can be put together to form routines.

Ball Routines: Children work in groups of four to eight. Using a circle, a square, a line or the formation of their choice, the children perform skills in a sequence determined by the members of the group. Routines may include synchronized individual skills or skills requiring group interaction or exchange of balls between children. The following sample routines are performed in a circle of six students.

Routine #1
(Simple)
1. Standing still do four consecutive one hand bounces (right hand).
2. Standing still do four consecutive one hand bounces (left hand).
3. Moving to the right, bounce the ball eight times.
4. Moving to the left, bounce the ball eight times.
5. Pass the balls across the circle to the person directly across from you (one bounce passes, the other passes in the air) and repeat four times
6. Repeat steps 1 to 5 several times.

Routine #2
(to music)
1. With two hands bounce the ball eight times to each beat of the music.
2. Continue for eight counts (bounces) bouncing the ball on every other beat.
3. Three circle members dribble to the center of the circle on the next four counts bouncing the ball on each count. On the next four beats they return to their starting place bouncing the ball on each beat. The other three in the circle bounce the ball eight times in place.
4. Repeat step 3 with the other three children dribbling in and out of the circle.
5. On the next four counts each child bounce passes his ball to the person on his right, one bounce pass for each count.

6. Repeat (four counts) step 5 bouncing the balls to the left.
7. Repeat the entire sequence of steps from 1 to 6.

Teaching Suggestions:

1. Ball routines are frequently best performed to music. The length of the routine can be determined by the length of the musical selection.
2. Children can create their own skills as well as their own routines.
3. Homogeneous groups make for more compatibility in developing routines.

Bamboo Hop Dance Routines: The tinikling skills presented in chapter 3 are appropriate for use in routines. Once children master the basic skills they can develop unique skills and a creative sequence of skills (a routine). Basic skills are presented on pages 35-37.

Lumey Stick Routines: Lumey stick routines can be developed by children using the skills presented on pages 27-29. Other original skills can be developed by children for use in their self-developed routines.

SUMMARY

In review, the routine is a unique combination of skills put together by the student. A routine is original to the student and can be used to provide enjoyment and to help children in overlearning skills. Other possible benefits of the routine are:

1. Routines give children the opportunity to create something unique to themselves.
2. Routines allow children to work within their own movement limitations. Children can select those activities in which they find success.
3. Routines provide the opportunity for the student to practice and follow an activity to completion. There is some satisfaction in saying "I developed that routine, learned it, and perfected it."

Some suggestions for effective learning using the routine are listed below:

1. Set a predetermined time limit or criterion for completion of the routine. In tumbling it may be several minutes while in Jumpnastics it would be four laps across the play area.
2. Once routines have been developed allow children to present their routines to other children.

3. Emphasize the selections of skills which the learner can do well. It is better to do simple tasks well than more complex skills poorly.
4. Routines can frequently be done to music to enhance the enjoyment derived from the activity.

Chapter 6

Inexpensive Equipment
for General Use

The following ideas do not relate to specific physical education activities but could be adapted for use in many different situations.

FIRE HOSE BOUNDARY LINES

In schools where there is no cement or asphalt all-weather surface, it is often difficult to get lines to stay on a playing area (i.e. grass or dirt). An idea which can be used quite successfully is the fire hose line. Many times, if requested, a fire department will donate old fire hose to the public schools. This hose when flattened and nailed (40 penny spikes) to the ground makes an excellent line (see illustration). An additional advantage is the fact that lime or chalk remains "white" on these lines much longer than on grass or dirt.

PLASTIC CLOTHESLINE BOUNDARY LINES

Another method of making boundary lines for use in physical education consists of a plastic clothesline stretched between 40 penny spikes. This clothesline is available from most hardware stores. The clothesline is simply wrapped around each spike (one wrap) and stretched to make the line taut. Spikes should be driven into the ground. The line should be tied around the spike at the beginning and end of the line. Advantages of this type of boundary line are: (1) availability of a large variety of colors, (2) its great mobility makes it easily adaptable for different activities, and (3) stretches rather than breaks with contact. *The rope must be fixed very close to the ground to prevent children from tripping during activity.*

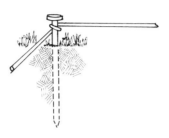

BOWLING PIN MARKERS

When lines are not necessary but a marker is desirable, such as in relays, bowling pins can be used. Most bowling alleys will give used pins to teachers (Note: Cardboard milk cartons can be used for the same purpose. See chapter 2).

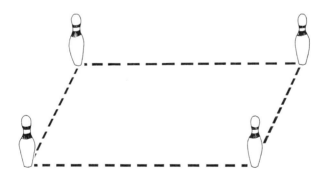

SOAP BARRELS FOR EQUIPMENT STORAGE

Laundries use large cardboard containers for storing laundry detergent. Frequently a teacher can get these lightweight barrels free when requested of local merchants. The barrels make excellent storage containers for use by physical education teachers.

TILE BASES

Frequently floor covering companies will have 9" x 9" or 6" x 6" tiles which do not match other tile patterns in stock. These are usually left-overs from a floor which did not require the full number of tiles antici-pated. Often the retailer will give such extra tiles to teachers. They make excellent bases for base tag, kick ball, softball, etc.

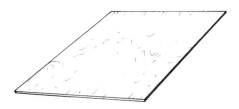

THE BALL PATROL[8]

The teacher of physical education is confronted with many clerical and technical duties which are truly not teaching assignments. One such duty, especially in the elementary school, is to care for and distribute equip-ment used during recess and other free play periods. This seemingly sim-ple duty can be quite time-consuming if handled in the ways traditional to many schools.

For example, it is not uncommon to find that in an elementary school with several classrooms, each class (or teacher) is assigned one basketball, one football, one softball, one rope, etc. The problems confronted in such a circumstance are numerous.

1.   First, each time a ball goes flat the teacher or class representative must seek out the physical education teacher to pump up the ball or, at least must go find the pump.

8. From Charles B. Corbin, "The Ball Patrol," *The Physical Educator,* 27 (1970): 134-35. Used by permission.

2. Secondly, when all children are not using the playground many balls and other pieces of equipment go unused while those children in play may be without adequate play equipment.

3. The physical educator, who probably will conduct classes at times other than recess, may be limited in terms of available class equipment because the balls and other equipment needed are spread throughout the school. Classes must be conducted with little equipment, or valuable time must be spent "rounding up" and returning balls to and from their respective home room.

4. Another consideration is the "home room" claim on a ball which may cause children to prohibit other children from using "their" equipment and even discourage between-class play interaction.

5. Finally, and perhaps most obviously, the chances of misplacing equipment assigned to home rooms are very real. Many balls are merely left on the playground or forgotten by those class members who "took them outside."

The *Ball Patrol* seems to be a reasonable solution to the problems suggested above. Most schools already have a safety patrol which uses the talents of students and, hopefully, develops educational goals as well. These safety patrol members are held in high regard by their peers, and indeed it is an honor to be named a patrol member. The *Ball Patrol* would be organized on the same basis as the Safety Patrol. The following procedures may be considered in organizing the activities of such a group.

1. Appoint two (or as many as needed) students, perhaps a boy and a girl, to be the ball patrol. This may be awarded as a reward for class achievements and be rotated from week to week.

2. Obtain containers for carrying the balls. Frequently, laundries will donate large cardboard cans or barrels which are lightweight and good for carrying equipment to and from the playground (see illustration).

3. Collection of *all* the equipment (balls, ropes, etc.) available in the school and locating them in one central place. This includes the "home room" equipment.
4. Having ball patrol members report to school early each morning. On arrival they count the pieces of equipment, pump up those balls in need of air, and report faulty equipment to the teacher.
5. The ball patrol distributes and collects *all* equipment during pre-school play, recess, and noon hour, in this way allowing more children to have more usable equipment. Also between-class play interaction is encouraged.

The ball patrol has worked successfully in many instances for those who have used it. It provides leadership roles for students, maximum use of equipment, more time availability for the teacher, and perhaps best of all, it provides maximum use of equipment for the physical education teacher in physical education classes. *Try it!*

Appendix

Index